The Bag Lady

The Bag Lady

Broken But Not Destroyed

Freda D. Blair

XULON PRESS

Xulon Press
555 Winderley Pl, Suite 225
Maitland, FL 32751
407.339.4217
www.xulonpress.com

© 2023 by Freda D. Blair

Cover Design by Jerome Lewis

All rights reserved solely by the author. The author guarantees all contents are original and do not infringe upon the legal rights of any other person or work. No part of this book may be reproduced in any form without the permission of the author.

Due to the changing nature of the Internet, if there are any web addresses, links, or URLs included in this manuscript, these may have been altered and may no longer be accessible. The views and opinions shared in this book belong solely to the author and do not necessarily reflect those of the publisher. The publisher therefore disclaims responsibility for the views or opinions expressed within the work.

Unless otherwise indicated, Scripture quotations taken from the King James Version (KJV) – *public domain.*

Scripture quotations taken from the Holy Bible, New Living Translation (NLT). Copyright ©1996, 2004, 2007 by Tyndale House Foundation. Used by permission of Tyndale House Publishers, Inc.

Paperback ISBN-13: 978-1-66288-346-0
Ebook ISBN-13: 978-1-66288-347-7

Contents

Dedication.................................... ix
Acknowledgments xi
In Loving Memory............................ xiii
Introduction xv
Chapter 1: In the Beginning 1
Chapter 2: No Means No........................15
Chapter 3: Unforgiving 21
Chapter 4: The Bags We Carry (Labeling) 25
Chapter 5: Just Thinking 31
Chapter 6: This Is Real.........................39
Chapter 7: Seasons of Pain 47
Chapter 8: I Used to Be a Victim, but I Changed My Mind 55
Chapter 9: Be It Resolved 63
Chapter 10: The Mind of Being Grateful...........73
About the Author 87

Dedication

This book is dedicated to my loving and caring family—Michael, my husband of 33 years, who continues to love and support me, and my four beautiful children, Michael II, Ryan, Kourtney, and Ambyr, for always being there and their unconditional love and support. I am so very proud to be your wife and mom. To my son-in-love Jordan, thanks for allowing me to love you and trusting me to be in your life. To my family, thanks for sharing me, always being there, your support, your forgiveness, and believing in me. You are my heartbeat!

Acknowledgments

I thank my Lord and Savior Jesus Christ, who birthed this Bag Lady in me. He is the reason for this book and the Broken Pieces Women's Annual Retreat Ministry.

To my friend (bestie) District Elder Sheila Blair, for your support, love, encouragement, and friendship for over 50 years! Love you, sis. Dr. (Overseer) Phyllis Foye, for always being that solid spiritual support, friend, and counselor, thank you. To Co-Pastor Markeida Johnson, thank you for being a friend, for your support, for the countless hours you spent helping me in editing this book and encouraging me all the way. I appreciate you! To Dr. Dottie Woods, my friend and motivator, who pushed me to write this book, I appreciate your push, motivation, and encouragement to author this book. To my sisters, Assistant Pastor Yolander Jackson, Deborah Brown, Joyce Carpenter, Yulonda Shannon and Minister Pearl Gordon, thanks for your support, respect, and always loving me. To the women of Broken Pieces Ministries, who have made it while broken. To those with a past of brokenness who were able to get through and help someone else. To those women who are not afraid to be transparent and say, "Yes, I am or have been broken but refuse to stay that way," to you who now know that you are *not* a victim, but *victorious* in Jesus Christ! I acknowledge you and continue to lift you in prayer. Thank you for inspiring me to continue!

In Loving Memory

My mother, my rock, my best friend, my pastor, and queen, the Honorable Pastor Marine B. Sharp. My stepdad, Deacon Willie Sharp; my grandmother, Sis Edna Mae Ferguson; my grandfather, Deacon Alonzo Ferguson; my brothers-in-love, Deacon Phillip Jackson and Bro Perry Gordon; nephew William Rawlings; my friend Pastor Rufus Woods; my best (pastor) friend Dr. Jackie G. Shannon, and two very special ladies in my life, District Elder Ann Davis, and Pastor Anna Pearson. I miss them dearly.

Introduction

This is a nonfiction book about the actions of those who cause us pain, their efforts, and who we can become as a result.

This book is about the baggage we carry from place to place, from relationship to relationship, from pain to pain, not even realizing what we hold or what's been given off as we pass by one another. I am writing about actions that happen in our lives that cause us to carry these things we call bags. How can we let go of these bags that caused us pain and headaches?

I pray that this book will help expose pain and brokenness in our lives. Take these pages and use them to help you understand that you can survive and that there is hope. My prayer is that you will take from this book the fact that you don't have to continue in the downward spiral that pain and unforgiveness will take you. Take my experiences and those around you to get clarity and know that this too shall pass. Prayer can change anything; it has changed me. Learn to pray about everything and watch God work things out for you.

My vision for my life has much to do with the pain from my past, and I envision helping other women that are hurting, abused, mistreated, raped, molested, or suffering from pain from within; whatever that pain is, I can see the Lord bringing healing and a fresh look on all of our lives. I can see this ministry that the Lord has blessed us to be a part of, to go to the next level, touching lives everywhere. I see this Broken Pieces Women's Ministry going from state-to-state healing and bringing life back to many broken women.

To see a woman smile that couldn't, to hear her laugh when she thought her joy was forever gone, to see the women crawl out of the pit they have been living in and become whole is a sight like no other. I pray for women with their many bags to look deep into those bags they carry and understand that they have a right to carry what they want, but know and understand that we have a choice in this world and we can choose how life will go! But remember you don't have to stay in the place you're in.

To see a change in the world of *women* is my passion, and to see it happen right before my eyes is a part of my vision.

Chapter 1

In the Beginning

My life started in January 1964, the day I came into this blessed world to the best mother that I could have had. I didn't say best parents because my parents were not married at my birth, so that makes me an illegitimate child. I have never said that out loud; it always sounded so bad because that meant that people would look at you differently. They look at a child that's illegitimate as a bad seed, one that's pushed aside, stepped on, abandoned, rejected, and left to survive on their own, all due to parents being unmarried or the father being absent.

My father was never a part of my life. I can remember very little about him, but he is the reason for some of my pain (and bags that I carried). Oh, how I wanted so badly to be a daddy's girl, one that he would take and cherish, hold and never let go, kiss hello and kiss goodnight; he would come to the school and be so proud of all the things I'd learned in my class, he would play outside with me and take me on a good ol' piggyback ride, take me to get ice cream and candy, and just be there to hold me for no reason at all.

That never was my life, but it doesn't hurt to dream. When I was seven years old, my dad as I knew him was gone, shot dead right beside the apartment that we lived in at that time. This was the very beginning of a new life, one that would change me forever.

This changed even my mom, who, by the way, was a drug abuser and had a boyfriend who was a drug pusher, who lived with us.

My mom really loved my dad, she told us, and when he was murdered, it really changed her for the better. She found a church and took us to it every week—it was the best thing that could have happened for us. My mom began to change right before our eyes. She stopped the drinking and drugs and began a Christian walk and never looked back. That changed our world as we knew it, but little did I know the changes were not over. A year after leaving that dreadful life that we lived, something we all dread would never happen to anyone happened to me.

We lived on a corner across from an old country store that we visited probably every day, so much so that they hated seeing us come to look at what they had (the same stuff they had the day before). This day, I went to the store and did what I always did: looked to see what they had and how much it was (as if the price changed from day to day). I saw that one thing I wanted more than anything:

the red Blow Pop sucker. I could never suck this sucker until it got down to the gum because I just couldn't wait that long to chew the gum and blow bubbles. Little did I know I was being watched by the nice, little old man that lived in the back of the store. As I write this, I wonder if he was the owner because he was always there and always watching to see what was going on. I never knew his name.

He saw me looking at the sucker, and as I left the store, he said, "Hey, you want this?" My eyes got big. I was really excited about what I was just shown: a red Blow Pop. He said, "I have more of them at my house right here in the back of the store." I followed Mr. No Name to his house in the back of the store. He really did have more, but I had to go all the way in to get them. Once I was inside, the "nice, little old man" told me he wanted something for what he gave me, but it wasn't money that he was after; it was my sweet innocence, my virginity, my honor, my little bitty eight-year-old life. I was never ever the same after that dreadful day. I never ate the suckers that day, and many, many years later I could never bring myself to eat those Blow Pop suckers. The pain was real.

I hid, I cried, but I vowed to never ever tell anyone because it was my fault. I was supposed to know better. I knew if I told that I would be beat, talked about, and put down, so I decided to never tell. I learned how to push things so far back into my mind it was as though those things never happened even if I'm standing right in it and it hurts, I would tell myself that it's not really hurting and

I'm ok. I taught myself that pain wasn't real, that I could push it all away.

I was guilty of sinning, of being a bad girl, of talking to a stranger. The guilt was too much, and I was ashamed of what had happened to me, of what I allowed to happen.

I went from blaming myself to asking myself where my mom was, my brothers, my sisters. Why didn't anyone care about where I was and what was happening to me? Why couldn't they see that I was in pain, that I needed help? Couldn't anyone see me?

I learned how to erect a wall or two or three depending on the level of pain that I was experiencing at the time.

I began to find bags to carry what I couldn't forget, carry what I didn't want to forgive, carry what I wanted to get someone else for, carry things that hurt so much that my mind couldn't hold them. I begin to pick up these bags that carried *everything* about me!

I became very quiet, a loner, afraid of many things and people. I became untrusting and skeptical that people cared or really wanted to be bothered with me; I always felt I was a burden to others, so I would always stand back out of the way, all the time wishing that someone knew or could feel this pain I was feeling. I lost track of where my pain stemmed from. Why was I such a loner, so bitter, so up and down, crying at the drop of a hat, just letting it go, but never wanting anyone to know that's what was going on?

In the Beginning

I can remember not liking me, not looking in the mirror, hating who I was. It was so overwhelming, always thinking that all men wanted was what had happened to me, feeling worthless.

I wished my dad was there to help me through this hard, horrible time in my life, but I felt so ugly and unwanted that it really didn't matter anyway.

Many years later, I realized that I really needed help. I then began counseling with a pastor and allowing myself to be totally transparent, telling them all that I had been through. Something that I had never done before. I began working through the things in my life that I was so afraid of and things that kept me from moving forward. Just looking in the mirror at myself was a huge deal, and as I was instructed to take my time and look at what the Lord had made. The scripture says in Psalm 139:14, "For I am fearfully and wonderfully made," and as I repeated this scripture to myself, it began to help me see myself a little differently. Then I was told to take selfies, and I was like, "Are you kidding me? Take a picture of me and like it?" This was a real hard one for me, but I began to do the things that I was asked, and I begin to see things start to change in my life.

This is during the time that I heard the Lord speaking to me about starting a women's ministry called The Broken Pieces Women's Retreat, and everything I was to do to get it started came flooding into my mind, including who I should have to be the speakers.

The Lord shared with me a play titled *The Bag Lady*, during this time and it was given to me to share with those who have been broken. It has blessed many. Before now, I had never even written anything down as to what I would say because I knew each time the Lord had someone to speak to, and He knew which way I needed to go. The play was never the same, but always ministered to someone watching, someone listening, and someone who had said within themselves, "I want out!"

There are some certainties in my life, and one is that our God is a healer. He is a miracle worker, He delights in healing His people, and He can do the impossible.

I believe that all of us have experienced some type of trauma in our life that leaves our minds deeply scared, and it causes us to constantly be re-victimized by our past.

We must get rid of all those past feelings, by revealing to God what we need Him to do, God wants to heal what we reveal.

Those feelings of hurt, distrust, lust, perversion, anger, shame, guilt, hatred, jealousy, bitterness, rejection, unforgivness, rage, fear, abandonment, and loneliness to name a few. These are feelings that torment us throughout our life if we don't acknowledge these feelings and seek help, we will continue in the same state of mine.

We are more alike than we know when it comes to hurt and pain. Unifying and shining light(reveal) on the feelings that create our own personal world of pain not only unifies the body of Christ but is a step in the direction of healing. God can heal the broken, but it's our responsibility to bring Him our pieces. Psalm 147:3 says, "He heals the brokenhearted and bandages their wounds."

Our Father is waiting for you to acknowledge that you have a problem or that something is wrong and then allow the Father or Doctor Jesus to fix what needs healing. He can do what no other doctor can do! He is The Healer!

I have learned that after you begin that walk of healing, the best thing you can do to heal faster and more completely is *forgive* the person that brought the harm to you in the first place! When you can forgive the person who has caused your life to go in a direction that you would not have chosen for your enemy, then you are truly getting somewhere. When you can forgive the person that was supposed to have protected you, that person that was supposed to have been your mentor—that coach, that uncle, that auntie, that cousin—or better yet those people who did that horrible thing to you that caused your life to spiral down out of control; that thing that caused you to treat others wrongly and not to trust anyone; that thing that made you question why you were even born; that thing that made you feel hopeless, uneasy, abandoned, rejected, a piece of nothing, you didn't even like who you were and couldn't stand to look at yourself, let alone have someone else looking at you; that thing that to this day you deal with and try to keep suppressed and in the back of your mind—when you can forgive that person that caused you such harm, then you get to be made *whole*! You get to help others and be used by our loving Father!

When we are hurting and just push the pain away instead of dealing with what hurts or why we're hurting in the first place, we end up a huge mess, or worse yet a hurtful mess. From this you begin to look for the wrong types of attention due to a need that you have.

Then when someone truly gives you an ounce of attention, you don't know what to do, and you become addicted to what is being handed to you, and all you want is more because all you've ever wanted is love, attention, and someone to acknowledge that you really exist, you're really human, you really can be loved, talked to, looked at, and even touched in a normal way. You find out that you can't even accept the very normal thing that you'd love to have because all this time you've lived an abnormal life, a life that has caused you to be stuck in the very place that you were when that thing happened to you. You get stuck there, and whoever did it to us becomes our life. We allow them to hold us hostage in that place of bondage, rejection, abandonment; of not being enough, not pretty enough; shame, guilt, loneliness; feeling that you and everything around you is dirty until you become OCD. This thing captures you and becomes your every move, your thoughts, what you will or won't do and what you will or can't deal with, it becomes your life, but in the stem of things we become very defensive, trying to keep from being hurt again. I'm sure you've heard the phrase, "Hurt people hurt other people"; this is such a true statement because when you've been hurt over and over, you vow to protect yourself at all costs.

People start to think of you as sharp or mean or nasty, but the fact of the matter is that you've been violated and things taken from you, and you didn't know how to do what needed to be done to take care of you and no one stepped in to help you, so you decided to protect yourself however you could.

There has been so much that I missed but didn't know I missed until the day I realized when I was molested, I shut down and never was the child I should or could have been. Then there were times that I felt I was missing something in my life but didn't know what it was until I realized it was real love, a mother's love.

I was twenty-one years old when my mother first touched me to hug me, but I remember seeing her hug and love on others. As a mother, I, too, didn't understand how to show real love, and so my kids suffered from all this pain that I bagged up and carried around with me.

Until you can be grateful for the feelings of not being enough, knowing that we have a God that is more than enough, you will never allow the God of all creation to multiply what you feel you're not, into what His plan is for you.

Everything that we have ever been through in our life is for the making of what He has planned for us to be. He is training us to be better, but at times it is a struggle, a hard place, a bitter pill to swallow, a painful situation, a breaking point; our God the Great I Am will step in and make us into that plan that He has for us. He works in those broken places, He loves to put pieces back together, to make it seem as if they were never out of place.

Who wouldn't serve a God like this? Only those that don't know Him to be a friend, a fixer of brokenness, and a mender of broken hearts! He's all that and so much more, more than we have space to even write. He is more than words can explain Him to be. He is!

There were so many bags that I carried, and I had no idea that they were even with me.

I taught myself how to not say a word, just look you over because I felt that all I ever got was a look and nothing else, so if looks could kill, you were sho'nuff dead after I was done with you.

I never knew how sharp my tongue could be and that I would hurt others by what I said because I also carried a nice "I love you" bag too, which disguised who I really was deep inside: very judgmental and afraid of being hurt. The things in my bags were deep hurt, deep pain, deep abandonment, deep rejections deep feelings of worthlessness. Through all this, I kept giving to those in need, trying to love people through stuff, not realizing that that was not real love. I wanted someone to notice who I was for once in my life, I would walk around as if my hands were raised saying don't you see me, "Don't you see that I am hurting? Don't you see that I need help. Don't you know that I have problems?" But there was no one to help me; no one saw me. I felt so invisible, so much so that even if you said I was attractive it was a lie in my mind.

There was no way that you saw anything over this way that was looking like anything anyone wanted. God guarded me even when I didn't know I needed to be guarded.

The bags that I carried were too painful to even acknowledge that I had them; I really didn't understand these bags until I began having this Broken Pieces Women's Retreat, which has blessed so many of us broken but not destroyed women.

We carry things around with us because we really don't realize that they are even there; we have gotten used to being who we are and don't know that there really is a better you waiting to step in at any given time. I am ever so grateful that the Lord allowed me to be the one to help other women that have been through similar things as myself. Many of the women that I speak with or share my testimony with have experienced worse things than I have, but it seems like the problems or issues that stem from the first onset are pretty much the same; we can all feel what the other was or is going through.

Look down and check to see which bag you're carrying with you right now. What's your state of mind, and how do you see yourself at this very moment? Many times, you will know what you are dealing with by how you see yourself now.

The Bag Lady

At one of our retreats, we had different bags filled with different issues, and you could choose to pick your own bag by either purchasing the bag or you may have been blessed for someone else to buy a bag for you. A young lady wanted a certain bag, and her mom, who was there with her, said, "I want to buy this bag and give it to my daughter." The point of this bag-purchasing session was to show that throughout our life, we have bags. Some we pick up, some are handed to us, some are generational curses, some we purchase, some we make ourselves, but they are all bags, and we carry them and we hold stuff in them and we sometimes don't want to depart from them because it's easy to keep what we are used to and not have to get familiar with something new—that is, called change. An un-Changed mind can keeps us in places that we don't like or agree with, and because we don't like change, we often just stay right where we are.

This young lady had picked a bag and wanted to be first to get hers, and her mom wanted to "bless" her, but the Lord gave me what to say to this young lady. I asked her why she wanted this bag and whether she knew what was in that bag that she wanted so badly. This young lady had lost her son years prior but had never spoken about that loss. She said, "Why do I have to talk about it? Why? I don't want to talk about it," and began to cry. This was the start of healing for her, and she was able to say a few things about her son that had never been voiced before, all because the Lord said, "Sell these bags, and add some pain inside the bags because these are the things we carry around with us from day to day." We don't look like what we are carrying with us. If someone asked to see what was in your bag, what would they pull out?

    I had all types of things in my bags. They started out small, but I carried them for so long and everywhere that I needed them to live by, and I fed them the lies that the enemy would tell me. I watched them grow with me. I started to hate the person I was, but I didn't know how to get rid of the bags that I carried. Rejection—that was one of my biggest bags. I was good to be friends with by boys at school, but that was only to use me to help with their girlfriend troubles, never good enough to be that special girl, I was always rejected told that she's not the one, I wanted to be friends with the girls but they talked about me because I didn't dress like they did. I was called names because I had big eyes. Loneliness crept its way right on in because I didn't have what others had and wasn't able to do what they did. My bags started early in life, and they grew the older I became and the more rejection, loneliness, and abandonment and the feelings of not fitting in, my bag became bags, and after while they grew heavier and increased in number until I didn't know what to do with who I was, and I didn't like me.

Chapter 1: "In the Beginning"

What's your beginning?

Journal here about what your beginning looked like. We all have one.

_____
_____
_____
_____
_____
_____
_____
_____
_____
_____
_____
_____
_____
_____
_____
_____
_____
_____
_____
_____

Chapter 2

No Means No!

We often find ourselves in sticky situations that cause us to feel as though we have no voice. I want you to know that we all have a voice, and what we speak should be taken as what is being spoken, especially in those sticky situations. Even if you first say one thing and then decide to change your mind, it should still be taken as it was given.

No means no.

Whenever you say no, it means no.

No matter what you ask me, if I say no, it's no. Don't give me candy after I tell you no; I don't want it. No means no.

If you ask me whether I want to spend the night, and I'm excited and ready, and you pick me up and bring me to your residence, but after I get there, I decide that I don't want to stay, that means exactly what I just said: no means no, period.

Life changes every day, and my mind may change at any time, allowing me to be me in the decisions that I want to make in my life. If I decide to be with you one day, and the next I change my mind, that means no, and I have every right to be me and make my own decisions.

Too often, people are taken advantage of because they decide to change their minds during something that they originally agreed to. Allow us to change our minds. You change yours.

Luke 15:17
"When he finally came to his senses, he said to himself, At home even the hired servants have food enough to spare, and here I am dying of hunger!"

This story in the Bible in Luke 15:17 is a very popular one. This is the Story of the prodigal son, who is known for wanting what was his too early. The son asked his living, healthy dad for his inheritance. He wanted it right now. The story goes on to say that the father gave his son what he asked for, and the son left home and went to a far country and spent all that his father had given him and found himself working in the pig's pen with the pigs, and he was starving so much so he gave thought to eating what the pigs were eating, but the Bible said that he came to himself (he changed his mind).

He thought about what he had back home. The story goes on to tell us that he went home, and the father received him with open arms. Even when we make huge mistakes and ask for things we have no business asking for, we still have every right to change our minds and say no. No still will mean no! No matter what you decide first, if you change your mind to something totally different, whatever your choice, no is still no! You get to change your mind: it's your right to do as you see is good for you, you can, simply say no.

What does your NO look like?
_____
_____
_____
_____

When your answer is NO, do you feel guilty?
_____
_____
_____
_____

What does your YES look and feel like?
_____
_____
_____
_____

Your thoughts and feelings:
_____
_____
_____
_____

Matthew 5:37 "But let your Communication be Yea, yea, Nay, nay."

"No" is a "negative used to express dissent, denial, or refusal, as in response to a question or request) not in any degree or manner; not at all" (Dictionary.com).

When considering the meaning of no, I realized that if someone asks me to do something that I don't desire to be a part of, and my response is no, and they continue to include me against my will, they either don't care, don't understand the English language, can't comprehend "no," or they enjoy inflicting pain on others.

This truth allows us to understand that many people living as we live must deal with distorted perceptions and need the Lord to help them see what is true.

We don't get to do whatever we want or what we feel to other people, especially when they have spoken the word *no*.

People who live like you, and I can perceive things very differently than we do.

I have heard, and I'm sure I have read somewhere that perception is the reality of what we believe to be true. So, people who hear "no" could really believe that they are hearing, "Yes, please keep it coming, go right ahead, and have it your way."

"Woe to those who call evil good, and good evil, Who put darkness for light, and light for darkness; Who put bitter for sweet, and sweet for bitter!"
Isaiah 5:20

No means no. Even at early ages, we see kids that don't understand the meaning of no. No matter how many times you tell them no, they still find themselves doing their own thing, or what they want to do.

**NO MEANS NO
SO, STOP ASKING!!**

You may even say things like "no, don't touch," "no, that's hot," "no, that will hurt you," "no, that's not a toy," "no, don't go down those steps," "no, don't open that cabinet," but they are bound and determined to do their own little thing. I say this because people start out learning how to do what they feel is right no matter what they are asked or commanded. They have their focus on what no means to them, and many times it means "yes, it's ok, if YOU want to, it means the other person involved has no say in what they intend on doing, it means that if I say no, then it doesn't need another input. It means they are saying yes, go right ahead, do to me as you well please, even if I'm saying NO DON'T, I DON'T WANT TO!!! None of that matters because they

Joshua 1:9 "Have not I commanded thee? Be strong and of good courage; be not afraid, neither be thou dismayed: for the Lord thy God is with thee withersoever thou goest."

have in their minds "no" really means to keep trying until you get what you want.

No means no!

No doesn't need me to explain why it's my answer! No is a whole totally complete sentence; it does not need justification or explanation.

Chapter 3

Unforgiveness

Unforgiving is being unwilling or unable to forgive or show mercy (Vocabulary.com). Unforgiving is also said to mean reluctant or refusing to forgive. When we hold on to unforgiveness, we allow no room for adjustments, errors, or weaknesses, and we are not allowing for shortcomings, especially in being harsh.

Sometimes we need to hear the words that we allow to come out of our mouths come right back to us to see if they are right to give out in the first place. We can say things that crush others for the rest of their life. At the same time, we feel we aren't unforgiving and that we aren't wrong in what we do or say to those who have hurt us or caused us any ill feelings. We think that they are just reaping what they sowed, and rightfully so.

Just so we can have a clear understanding of what it is that we are really doing and feeling, I looked at the word *unforgiveness* and the synonyms for it: cruel, heartless, relentless, ruthless, unrelenting, pitiless, remorseless, revengeful, uncompassionate, unsympathetic, and so on. These words come with many feelings, and I'm sure you may see yourself now or what you were before you forgave.

As mentioned in the earlier chapters, I was molested at the age of eight, and I felt the pain from this for many years. This thing held me in bondage, and I wasn't able to be the person I was meant to be because I was so angry, bitter, and vengeful. I wanted to be able to get this dude back; I wanted to inflict the pain on him that he inflicted on me. I wanted him to suffer, and I would think of the things that could cause him pain and wish in my heart that I would be allowed to inflict this on him. But God, He never allowed me to do such a thing, He is all about forgiving as He forgave us.

Chapter 3: "Unforgiving"

Journal about someone that you have unforgiveness toward.

Chapter 4

The Bags We Carry (Labeling)

The bags we carry often come from what we know now as being labeled. We have been marked by family, friends, teachers, pastors, the point-your-fingers-at-others saints, the nice-nasty neighbors, the bullies, the nasty girls, the I-only-want-you-for-what-you-got dudes, the abuser who tells you it's your fault, the peacock who walks around with their head up in the air looking down on you like you're the scum of the earth, and those who knew but never lifted a hand to pull you out.

Life can beat you down even though you haven't started your life! All those people could have made a better decision on your behalf but chose to do their own thing with you.

Those who never gave thought to what the outcome of what they did or said to you are those selfish folk; sometimes they are those who have been hurt themselves and want someone else to feel their pain.

The Bag Lady

The labeled bags come when we can't see anything but negative in our lives, when we believe all the lies we've been told.

We look in the mirror and tell ourselves we are nothing and nobody because of our labels. When we pattern our lives after the pain in our hearts, we make mistakes, and others won't allow us to live them down.

We all have a choice in life; that's why God created us the way He did!

We get to choose the life we want to live, good or bad, right or wrong, fast or slow. We get to decide if we will do what our parents did or do otherwise; we get to decide if we will be happy or sad. We determine if we will get revenge on the one who hurts us or forgive them and let it go. Forgive them and set yourself free.

We can choose to be the best we can be. You must not allow your past hurts, pain, disappointments, or sufferings to be your guide. You must take those things as steppingstones to step into the person you want to be.

All this happens to make you a better you, not to keep you down. It all happens to allow you to know that "Greater is He that is in me than he that's against me." If God is for you, who can be against you? God has been there the whole time. He will never leave you, nor will He forsake you, and you will be able to begin to see that new you because "no weapons formed against you shall prosper." Remember that people or weapons that have formed to kill you, can say and do whatever they will, but neither the people nor weapons can't prosper or complete what it was sent out to do.

Yes, they said it; yes, they did it: and yes, they meant what they said and what they did, but you must understand clearly that they did not know who you were then and the person that God created you to be. I Peter 2:9 "But you are not like that, for you are a chosen people. You are royal priests, a holy nation, God's very own possession. As a result, you can show others the goodness of God, for He called you out of the darkness into His wonderful light."

God has not made us, created us, and formed us to be what others say we are; we are everything God has said we are. We can do the things that He said we can do, and there is nothing and nobody who can stop us but us.

Others can hinder, but they can't stop the plans. Jeremiah 29:11 states, "For I know the plans I have for you, says the Lord, plans to prosper you and not to harm you, plans to give you hope, and a future." Yes, He promised to strengthen you, to give you rest, to take care of all your needs, God promises to answer your prayers, God promised to work everything out for you. God promised to be with you always, God promised to protect you, God promised freedom from sin, and there are so many more promises of God, so why don't' you just let go of the negative affirmations and carry the label of being my Father's child?

I am truly blessed because God loves me and cares about what I care about; He is working things out for me.

He is answering my prayers so that I will not be consumed by the things of this world. I will move beyond the labels that were placed on and over my life. Today is the day of salvation, and I have decided to move on from this place that I allowed to take complete control of my life.

I will no longer walk with my head down; I will look to the hills from which my help comes. I will no longer feel like I am out of place for my Father has spoken to me that "wherever my foot is placed, it belongs to me."

I am walking on what belongs to me. I will no longer feel that I am not enough, for He has said, "We are His workmanship created in Christ to do good works, which God had before ordained that we should walk in them." As stated in Ephesians 2:10 and in Romans 3:23, "For all sinned and come short of the glory of God" Therefore, whoever has wrongly labeled me has come from the same side I come from. In other words, no one is any better than the other, so how can I look at anyone as though I am better? Label me if you must, but God has not let me stay that way. I may have been exactly what you said I was, but God came that I would not stay the way I came. I will not be stuck any longer in the labels of this world.

See me now but not for long because I am working toward my eternal home. I am what God says I am. I am labeled in Christ Jesus!

Galatians 4:7: "Wherefore thou art no more a servant, but a son; and if a son, then an heir of God through Christ."

John 15:11: "These things have I spoken unto you, that my joy might remain in you, and that your joy might be full."

Ephesians 1:3: "Praise be to God and the Father of our Lord Jesus Christ, who has blessed us in the heavenly realms with every spiritual blessing in Christ."

Romans 8:38–39: "For I am convinced that neither death nor life, neither angels nor demons, neither the present nor the future, nor powers, neither height nor depth, nor anything else in all creation, will be able to separate us from the love of God that is in Christ Jesus or Lord."

These are a few of the reasons that I will no longer allow what others say about me be my name or my label but will from now on be labeled by the one that created me, formed me, made plans for me, loves me unconditionally, and is waiting for me to do what is right to make it where He is. Thank you, Jesus, for labeling me as one of Yours.

2 Corinthians 6:18: "And I will be a Father to you and you shall be sons and daughters to Me."

Chapter 4: "The Bags We Carry (Labeling)"

Journal about the labels that you know you picked up along your journey of life.

_____
_____
_____
_____
_____
_____
_____
_____
_____
_____
_____
_____
_____
_____
_____
_____
_____
_____
_____
_____
_____

Chapter 5

Just Thinking

There are so many things in our life that has and will continue to cause us to be hindered or have setbacks, but it is entirely up to us to either allow those things to take place or fight back with the Word of God that was left here that we would use it for His glory and as a weapon against the enemy.

Many people have experienced either what you have or worse. The enemy has often talked so harmfully to us that we have decided within ourselves that we will never share about the ordeal that we have had to live with or through. We get to be examples for the Lord for He chose us to go through our hardships and be healed, maybe even to help others who are still going through their own hardships.

The Lord knew that you would go through this and come out a winner; we are not victims, but we are *winners*. We have been through some challenging places in life, but those places don't define who we are, nor do they stop us from being who we desire to be. We are who God said we are, and we can very well be who He said we can be, and there is no one on this side of glory that can stop the will of God that is on our life!

We are more than conquerors through Jesus Christ! The Bible says, in II Timothy 1:7, "For God hath not given us the spirit of fear; but of power, and of love, and of sound mind." We have love to give, and love is coming back to us; we must believe that we have a sound mind, one that knows how, knows when, knows where, knows what, and knows how long we must use what has been offered to us.

I Corinthians 10:13
"There hath no temptation taken you, but such as is common to man: but God is faithful, who will not suffer you to be tempted above that ye are able; but will with the temptation also make a way to escape, that ye maybe able to bear it."

He is our everything, and He wants us to make it. He wants us to be victorious, not failures. He supplied our needs and placed in each of us the very thing we need to get through whatever we are in. He made a way of escape for every one of us; we must look to Him, who knows what we need!

He is a friend and a father, an encourager, a healer, and a way maker, and He wants what's best for each of us. There is nothing we can't do with what we have to use (Jesus). The words to a old hymn says it this way,

"It is no secret what God can do
What He's done for others He'll do for you.
With arms wide open He'll pardon you;
it's no secret what God can do.

He gets pleasure in helping us when we are at a low, weak place in this life.

Remember that we go through things so that He will get the glory when we come out of the thing we have been allowed to be in; knowing that we are not going through this alone makes it even more worth it.

God has looked at us and said that we could go through every single trial, tribulation, test, abuse, rejection, abandonment, divorce, job loss, breakup, failure, injury, sickness, natural disaster, loss of a loved one, and the list goes on and on and on. But not just go through these things, but come out looking like we never were in any of them. For the Lord will get the glory out of what we come out of. All the things that were supposed to have killed you and didn't, He will get the glory. Those things you went through when you were young are your steppingstones to get you closer to Jesus and to build a better you.

The Lord knew He could depend on you and that you would make it out of your Egypt; He knew that though He slay me, we would trust Him. He knew that the pit would only be a holding spot for a better place, that your dungeon was a step down to look up. We know now what we didn't know then and that is our God is an awesome, all-knowing, all-seeing, and ever-present God who can do what no other power can do!

He had a plan the whole time; we just needed to walk in the plan of God! Jeremiah 29:11: "For I know the thoughts I think toward you, saith the Lord, thoughts of peace, and not of evil, to give you an expected end."

He expected me to come out of what I was in, He expected me to push through the mess, He expected me to go through the storm, He expected me to see myself as He sees me and know that with Him I can!

We start separating who we are by putting those things we don't like about ourselves, don't want to share about ourselves, want to forget about ourselves, and then those things that happened to us—good and evil we file those away and they grow into bags. We handle and hold them as if they are a real part of us, not realizing that we are only holding on to the past and can't change a thing that's in the bags we carry. Until we release the pain, hurt, brokenness, or past trauma, we will never be the best of ourselves! Just let your past go, forgive those who hurt you, and watch your life change right before your eyes.

"New Life"

Colossians 3:10: "Put on your new nature, and be renewed as you learn to know your creator and become like Him."

By letting it all go and forgiving the abuser, I set myself free! Freedom can look good on you; just do it!

We continue throughout our life to place our hurts into bags. Whatever happens to us, we just add something new to our bag and keep moving like this is what you do.

When you find Mr. or Mrs. Right, you tend to hide who you really are until something triggers the pain inside because you want what you have even though they don't know the real you until after you say, "I do!" Both of you bring all your luggage that you've been carrying and separating all your life to your new residence. Then the day arrives that you begin unpacking all the hurt, pain, mistrust, abandonment, and rejection, and you have no clue who you are or the person you married is either, because both of you have bags that you've hidden for most of your life. Now the new life has caused you to see the real you!

Bags are genuine, if we don't get help, we will repeat, damage, or destroy the life we have been blessed to have!

These bags can permanently be changed to what you've dreamed about; these bags don't have to carry what your life dealt you. You can change the route that you're on today. You get to be better, the best, and you get to say

Philippians 4:13
"I can do all things through Christ which strengtheneth me."

how you feel and how you will react or act. You get to decide what happens in your next chapter or what you want to have in your bags. It's up to you to be a healed you, a better you. Life is too short to deal with what you hate about yourself. Change it; God has given us the gift of choice, and I choose to be better. I prefer to no longer be in pain from my past or allow my past to dictate my future. No, you don't get to continue to mess up my life, not after I found out that that's what is going on. I have the power to change to say, "Not today, Devil! I get to be, and I get to do and I get to make the decisions of how my life will be. With the help of my Lord and Savior, I can, and I will! Watch out world, here I come, a better me!

II Timothy 1:7 "For God has not given us the spirit of fear; but of power, and of love and of a sound mind."

Chapter 5: "Just Thinking"

What is on your mind today?

Chapter 6

This Is Real

The overwhelming feeling of not understanding who or why you even exist. Trying to understand if there is a God and why He would allow these horrible things to happen to you.

What is the purpose of so much pain in the heart of a human being? Why would God allow you to feel this much pain? There were so many questions about why, how, or what I did to deserve such a punishment; how do these types of things happen when you're just a child? Don't adults look after kids, protect them, help them, and keep them out of harm's way? They are not supposed to cause the harm that changes your life for the worst and even jacks up your adult life; it's devastating to be a part of something surreal!

You get a feeling of not fitting in anywhere; you feel that you are the problem, that you are a bother to people, even those you feel should love you.

Before we acknowledge our trauma, we feel as though no one sincerely has our back. We didn't grow up having anyone loving us unconditionally.

You don't trust anyone, and it makes you feel hopeless, uneasy, abandoned, and rejected; you don't even like who you are and can't stand to look at yourself, let alone have someone else looking at you.

To this day, you deal with things from your past, trying to keep things suppressed and back in your mind—the triggers that will (if you allow them to) hold you back.

When we are hurting and push the pain away instead of dealing with what hurt us or why we're hurting, we end up a huge mess–a hurtful mess.

Going forward, we begin to look for the wrong type of attention due to what has transpired in life, and we find ourselves feeling very vulnerable.

We also deal with this problem when someone truly gives us an ounce of positive attention, we don't know what to do because we have been so addicted to the dysfunction that we have been acquainted with. All we really want is more positive attention because we are seeking to be loved.

We realize that all we ever wanted was an everyday life, to move from the place of where that thing happened, to a better place. We get stuck there, and whoever did it to us becomes our life. We allow them to continue to hold us hostage in that place of pain. This thing captures us and becomes our whole world, our every move and thought; it dictates what you can or can't do, what you like and dislike, what you will or won't deal with, how you function from day to day, how you see others, how you treat your friends, and family. It decides how you act or react to all situations that you have in your life and puts us in what feels like a strait jacket.

Hurt People Hurt Other People

Due to the pain, we find ourselves being very defensive, trying to keep from being hurt again. I'm sure you've heard the saying, "Hurt people hurt other people." This is such a true statement because when you've been hurt over and over, you get to a bitter place, and you tell yourself that no one else will hurt me again. You feel that no one else covered you, but the one that should or could was the one that inflicted the pain, so you vow that no one else will ever hurt you. You decide that you will get them before they could ever get you.

Then you get labeled "sharp tongued," that you cut people with your words or that you are just plain old mean and nasty, when that's not it at all; you've been violated! Things have been taken from you, so you didn't know how to do what needed to be done to take care

Isaiah 40:31: "But they that wait upon the LORD shall renew their strength; they shall mount up with wings as eagles; they shall run, and not be weary; and they shall walk, and not faint."

of you, and it seems that no one stepped in to help, so therefore you decided no more (the exposure was too much).

When I realized I had been molested, I never knew how much I missed in life because I shut down and never was able to be the child I should or could have been. For many years I felt the void in my life. At first, I didn't know what it was, only to find out later in life that it was the fact I was missing the love from my parents.

Yes, as I am finding out that many of us missed parental love, I can remember like it was yesterday. I was twenty-one years old the first time my mom hugged me, but the most hurtful part is that I remember seeing her hug and love on others before she ever shared with me. So as a mother to my own children, I didn't understand how to show genuine love. My kids suffered from all this pain that I held on to, bagged up, and carried around with me. I thank God that my mom gave me all that she had at that time. I understand very clearly now that you can't give more than you have been given until you understand that there is more to give and learn how to give it to those who are in need.

If you've never been loved or shown how, then how can you give love away? You can't demonstrate what you've never been taught. If you don't know, how can you do better?

Everything that we have ever been through in our life is for the making of what He has planned for us to be. He is training us to be better, but at times it is a struggle (the struggle is real), a hard place, a bitter pill, a painful situation, a breaking point that seems to have no fix to it and no purpose for it. It's then that our God, the Great I Am, will step in and help us walk in the plan that He has for us. He works in those broken places. He loves putting pieces back together to make it seem like they were never out of place. Who wouldn't serve a God like this? Only those who don't know Him for themselves. God is a fixer of brokenness and a mender of broken hearts, and He gets pleasure in helping us. He's all this and so much more, more than we have space to even write; He is more than words can explain Him to be. Just remember that whatever you need, He is!

The Tongue Will Hurt Others

I never knew how sharp my tongue was and never realized that I would hurt others with what I said because I had camouflaged it with an "I love you" bag and an "I would give you the shirt off my back" bag. These two bags that I used to disguise my hurt, were what I thought love was; as long as I was giving you something, I was showing you my love.

I have learned that our mouths can be deadly, but they can be so pleasant and so very sweet; it's all up to us to speak those things that are worth hearing, those things that will promote better behavior, to help others be better and not add more negativity to their life.

Proverbs 18:21: "Death and life are in the power of the tongue: so therefore, we can speak life, or we can speak death, we can help others live or we can kill them all with the words that we decide to come from our mouths… Let us speak life and help others move forward."

Healed From My Bag of Negativity

I thank God for Jesus Christ who died to heal me from all the bags of negativity that surrounded me all my life. He came that I would be free from within, and though I can't tell you the day or the time, I know that Jesus has fixed me from so many things that I had going on inside of me by showing me myself, and I am forever grateful! He began by telling me to pray, and I would pray about what He allowed me to see in me, and I would fast and pray until that thing was gone. Then there were things that I knew were there, and I knew that they were not like Jesus, so I would ask the Lord to help me and save me from anything that wasn't like Him, Lord, I trust you with me; mold me and make me over today.

Psalm 34:6: "This poor man cried, and the Lord heard him and saved him out of all his troubles." This spoke directly to me. I am not perfect or all together yet, but I am under construction, being fixed, and working on me each day. I thank the Lord that I am not what I was, and I am working hard to be what He's calling for me to be each and every day. This is a process, and yes, it takes time, but don't give up; keep pressing and keep pushing, and we can make it if we continue and stay consistent.

Chapter 6: "This Is Real"

Journal about things that people tried to make you feel weren't real in your life.

_____
_____
_____
_____
_____
_____
_____
_____
_____
_____
_____
_____
_____
_____
_____
_____
_____
_____
_____
_____

Chapter 7

Seasons of Pain

When you are in a place of hurt, you seem to learn really quickly how to nurse it, feed it, pamper it, hold it, talk to it, pat it, believe it, have a pity party with it, and just be complacent where you are with your stuff. This was life as I knew it, and this to me, was better than just letting it go and being healed. Then you deal with the fear of someone knowing that you were abused. With all the work, tears, and talk you've had right here, why would you think about doing anything else? Maybe there's a fear of letting that baby (pain, hurt, etc.) go and knowing that if you do you will have to find a new way of dealing with yourself, and we know that dealing with ourselves has been a task. You don't want to deal with who you are but expect others to deal with you and your buffoonery (Sis Maria's words); this is how I expected people to deal with who I was, but I didn't like me and my buffoonery.

This word *buffoonery* goes well with who we become during this time in our life because sometimes we refuse to be helped, and we think we know more than the ones that know how to help us out of our buffoonery (I give you permission to laugh out loud on that one). Thinking about my past, when I allowed myself to stay in that mindset, things would continue to visit my mind, and I continued to have seasons of pain. These seasons became so familiar that they were a common place for me.

Every year around the same time, I would be so sad, crying and not understanding what I was feeling or crying about. I could not calm my own tears because they were from deep inside, and the feeling was real but unknown to me. I felt so bad at times I just wanted to escape the pain any way possible. I continued to question myself about the feelings, my emotions, my breakdowns. These episodes came around the same time that my dad was murdered and close to the time I had been molested, so I had pushed all these emotions to the back of my mind, but they were still pushing their way through, and I wasn't aware of what was going on inside of me. The feelings of loss, abandonment, rejection, unwantedness, hurt, pain, and some other emotions that were unexplainable were my best friends. They kept me company; they seemed to know what to say every day; they ate breakfast, lunch, and dinner with me; they kept me from talking to others; they kept me isolated, secluded and feeling lonely; they kept me wishing that someone could see me; they kept me looking at myself as though I didn't deserve to even be alive. These seasons that I continued to live in kept me crying, sad, frustrated, annoyed, irritated, and so many other feelings of just not wanting to really exist because I had those friends (emotions) that kept feeding me negative things that had happened in my life.

I revisited the pain and the situations and tried to see what I had done wrong, how bad of a person that I was that no one wanted to be bothered, why I wasn't good enough for this world that I lived in.

I thought about why life was so terrible, why I wasn't cute enough, why was I the laughingstock of the class, and why no one picked me. My mind was full of the negative version of what I felt about myself.

I didn't know why and what God had created until I read Psalm 139:14, which says, "I will praise thee; for I am fearfully and wonderfully made: marvelous are thy works; and that my soul knoweth right well." This enlightened me that He says I'm good and I am enough!

I was controlled by revisiting the molestation and the cruel words uttered so many times in my life, to the words that I would never be anybody and I would never make anything of myself, the words that we were trash, that my family wasn't worth loving. We grew up very poor; we didn't have heat or food at times. Clothes were hand-me-downs three times over, and we took turns on being the next one in line to get shoes. My mom did her very best being the mother of ten, and of the ten seven living children she raised by herself.

My mom was married to a man who rode off into the sunset (that's what we always said, anyway) and never looked back. She then had a boyfriend that was a drug dealer, and he lived with us and sold drugs from our apartment. My mom was addicted to drugs herself, to the point that I witnessed her doing drugs in her arms through her veins (shooting up). She would drink and party, and we had many visitors in and out of our apartment. I remember being asleep and my mom pulling us to the floor because someone was shooting through our windows.

So, you relive those nightmares of the abuse and neglect, and then you live to hear others tell you who you are and what you will never be. You just sit back and agree with what has been said to you because you already feel rejected and isolated, and this all hinders you from being able to be the friend, wife, husband, sister, brother, or whoever you were supposed to be. Until you change your mind, you will never change. This all reminds me of the lyrics to an old song titled "Change Has Come Over Me, He Changed My Life and Now I'm Free." This song rings true in my life: God brought me out of the misery that I was stuck in for over forty years. God changed my life when I decided to change my mind! Your whole life will change when you change the way you see or perceive things with the help of the Lord.

I thought I was a misfit; I felt that I wasn't good for anything. I thought I was a nobody, and I felt that no one cared, but when I decided to change my mind, I began to realize that my Father in Heaven had already spoken over my life and that He had a plan for me no matter what others had said. He had the first and last say over my life, and I began to keep my focus on what my Savior and my King had spoken over me. I will believe the report of the Lord. He said I am His daughter, and I will walk in that.

He Spoke (God)

He said I am somebody.
He said I can do all things.
He said I am above and not beneath.
He said I can live, He spoke those things to me.
He said all things are possible.

He said to be not conformed to this world
but be transformed by the renewing of your mind.
He said I can change my mind.
He said that I can be an overcomer.
He said I am a winner not a loser.
He said I have the *victory*.
He said I am a new creature.
He said I am healed.
He said I am strong.
He said I am forgiven.

He said I am made whole.
He said I am adopted into the royal family.
He said I am His and He is mine.
He said I am fearfully and wonderfully made.
He said I am worth it!

There is not one thing that we can't do with the help of Jesus Christ, for He is everything to each of us, and you can. Believe it. He is my *everything*,
And I won't take it back.

That is why I bless the Lord at all times and His praise shall continually be in my mouth. (Psalm 34:1)

Even when I don't feel like praising Him, I will
bless the Lord.
Even when I'm sick, I will bless the Lord.
Even when I don't agree with the outcome, I will
bless the Lord.
At all times His praises shall continually be in my mouth!
I have had many seasons filled with pain, and seem like it was never going to end, but even then, I continued to bless the Lord through all my pain, and He saw me through it all! And I didn't lose my mind!!
Every season has to change, keep looking forward to the changing of your season.

Chapter 7: "Seasons of Pain"

Journal about all the different seasons of pain that you have suffered through.

Chapter 8

I Used to Be a Victim, but I Changed My Mind

I used to be a victim, but I changed my mind. Many of us have chosen to live with a victim mentality. Merriam-Webster defines it as the belief that one is always a victim: the idea that bad things will always happen to one. WebMD states it as someone with a victim mentality claims that everything that happens to them is the fault of others. It may be the fault of their family member, coworker, or friend. They constantly complain about the dreadful things that happen in their lives. They don't take any responsibility, asserting that the circumstances aren't in their control.

This was I or me or us. I would always mention what I went through to get others to feel my pain and to know that I had a lousy life. Terrible things had happened to me, and they needed to understand that I hurt and "poor me." Although I really did have bad things, even awful things happen to me throughout my childhood and into my adulthood, it wasn't necessary to constantly play the victim. I played the victim very well, and as a victim, you also know whom to tell all your craziness to and who will listen and who won't. I think now it was a "pat me on my back" game because life wasn't fair to me.

When you have a victim mentality, you have dealt with trauma and horrific things have happened to you, and many are ashamed to tell anyone what really happened to them, so they play the victim card instead. As victims, we don't know how to cope with what's real in our lives; we only know how to be the victim, and the thought of change brings fear and much doubt that things could actually be better. This victim mentality causes us to be very defensive, thinking that everyone is against us. This is hazardous, painful, and lonely, and we wonder why people don't want to be a part of our pity party. We tend to blame everyone else for the dysfunction in our life. According to WebMD, the following are examples of someone with a victim mentality:

- You blame others for the way your life is.
- You think life is against you.
- You have trouble coping with problems in your life and feel powerless against them.
- You feel stuck in life and approach things with a negative attitude.
- You feel attacked when someone tries to offer helpful feedback.

- Feeling bad for yourself gives you relief or pleasure.
- You attract people who blame others and complain about their life.
- It's difficult for you to examine yourself and make changes.

I could see how I was so messed up in my mind; I could see me doing many of these examples when I was going through this victim mentality season in my life. This brings back so many memories. I now look forward to all these things not being a part of my life any longer; I want to be and stay free from my past. (My past is not my future.) I have learned many things in this short life of mine, and some of the most important things that keep me grounded are that I can choose to be, to be sad or happy, to love or not to love, and to be a troublemaker or a peacemaker. I have learned through a lot of mistakes and pain that this is all up to me. I choose to serve the Lord, I choose to be victorious, and I choose to be the better me and leave the old me in my past because I found out that I get to be happy, I get to be loved, I get to walk up rightly before our Lord. I get to talk right, be right, live right. I get to be held accountable for my actions, I get to have joy, and I get to forgive all those who caused this painful past. I get to love them and be happy about who I am becoming, and all this is because Jesus promised me that He would never leave me or forsake me and that He would change me if I wanted to be changed.

This life we are in is a choice that the Good Lord has given us, and I choose to do it all the way right with His help. I can't be or do anything without Him!

Thank the Lord I no longer have to be a victim; now I call myself *victorious* in Jesus Christ. He has brought me out of the mind that I was once in. He has given me a reason to say, "Lord, I just want to thank You." He has turned my life all the way around to be a better me. I am really liking and enjoying the person that He is making me into. I am not finished yet, so please, if you see me down here not doing it the way the Bible says (not what you or someone else says), then by all means help a sista make it in!

It's a choice, and it's really up to you to decide what you want for your life. I got tired of negative me, so I traded her in for a positive me. You too can make a trade of your life by telling the Lord that you don't like who you are and that you want to change. You can really be detailed when you talk to Him too; tell Him that you don't like your actions or reactions, that you don't like the way you think. Maybe you are one of those people we call stinking thinkers who only can see the bad and never even try to see any good in themselves or anyone else.

I know there is good in all of us, and the Word of God is a witness to this fact. I Timothy 4:4 states, "For every creature of God is good, and nothing is to be refused if it is received with thanksgiving." I just want to tell the Lord Thanks for what He has for you; I thank Him in advance for what He is going to do for you! He is waiting for you to choose what type of life you want for you.

This is now in your hands, and it's your choice what you decide to do with your life. No one can do you but you, and no one can be you but you. Stop allowing people to measure who and what you are or will become. Don't allow forty of your good years to be wasted being a victim of what happened to you because all the things that happen in your life come to make you better, and to help someone along the way that need to know that God is able to help them as He helped you, these things didn't and don't come to break us (unless you need to be broken) or kill us. We are not victims, but we are who He said we are, we are more than conquerors! Remember that all that we go through comes that we would be a witness to His goodness and His mercy and His healing and so much more; we are created for His glory. He allows us to go through things so that we will tell someone that the Lord was there for us when we went through that same situation, and if He did it for us, He will and wants to do it for you. There is nothing that our God cannot do; He can handle all our problems big or small.

He knows all things, and what you're going through is no surprise to Him. He knew before you that it would happen, and He knew what you would go through and that you would make it out, so even if you're not out yet, you can witness that you didn't lose your mind, that you didn't turn back, and that you know without a doubt that the Lord had to take you through this. This is how he gets the glory from your situation. He knows how to turn your world around and make your life seem to be brand new.

There is nothing that our God cannot do; He can do anything but fail! I am so glad that about nine years ago, I decided to take that step toward Jesus, and He allowed me to walk to Him and be changed. I am so glad that He allowed me to be fixed. He allowed me to be a witness for Him. He allowed me to go through the things that I had to go through to be who I am today. Always remember that if you're still alive, He's not finished with you yet.

Thank You, Lord, for seeing in me those things that I couldn't see until You began the transformation in me. Get the mind of Christ and be an overcomer and watch the transformation in your life. He will allow you to see the things about you that you've never seen.

These were the seasons of my pain, a victim mentality, a mind not pleasing to God, and so much pain that I was totally broken, but God sent His Son to mend the brokenhearted, to set the captive free, to loose chains that may have us bound, to transform the creepy crawly worm into a beautiful butterfly—a better me and a better you! The seasons must change, and it's time for your next season. Change me, oh Lord!

Remember that when you become that beautiful butterfly from that ugly, nasty caterpillar, the butterfly never goes back to a caterpillar, so you must keep pushing, keep flying, keep becoming. Fly high and He will be right there with you throughout every one of your seasons.

Chapter 8: I Used to Be a Victim, but I Changed My Mind

Journal about the victim that you were and how you changed to the victorious person you are today.

_____
_____
_____
_____
_____
_____
_____
_____
_____
_____
_____
_____
_____
_____
_____
_____
_____
_____
_____
_____
_____

Chapter 9

Be It Resolved

Everything the enemy meant for my bad and every person he sent my way to kill me, be it resolved, didn't work. I look at what the forefathers did, and I repent for their sin that may have caused me to pick up the wrong bag, be it resolved. I forgive my grandmother for mistreating my mother, for neglecting her and not loving her as a mother should, which caused my mom not to feel loved, nor did she know what love looked like, be it resolved. I forgive my parents for not doing the proper thing by getting married before conceiving me out of wedlock and causing the feelings of rejection and abandonment to be a part of my life, be it resolved. They didn't cover me as a child, or as their child, their baby girl, and left me so that the world could teach me what I need in my life. Be it resolved.

The Bible tells us in Proverbs 22:6, "Train up a child in the way he should go: and when he's old, he will not depart from it." If we train a child up in the way he needs to go, he will still know the way when he grows up. My parents taught me that it was ok to have sex before marriage and have children without a spouse. They also taught abandonment and that it's ok to reject people and not trust them. They taught these things by the way they lived their lives, but I thank the Lord that I didn't follow their footsteps in those things.

They taught me how to keep a distance, guard myself, guard my heart from those closest to me. They taught that it's ok not to be touched, hugged, kissed, or to show affection to your loved ones. They taught me that it's ok if you don't express your feelings of love, it's ok to just assume your child is ok, never checking to see if that's the case or not, and that its ok not to protect your child. Be it resolved that I forgive my parents for all the hurt and pain that they caused me because I understand now that they could not give me what they had never received themselves. They didn't know how to love me or know how to be loved; they could only provide me what they had. Remember, unless the Lord helps us, we will never be healed from what has happened to us in our past. I forgive you. Be it resolved.

Life has a way of dealing cards that seem so unfair and so wrong, but the truth be told, God still has a plan. As Psalms 139:16 says, "You saw me before I was born. Every day of my life was recorded in your book. Every moment was laid out before a single day had passed." Remember that no matter what has happened to us, He has a plan, even through all your pain, hurt, wrongs, abuse, conflict, problems, issues, abandonment, rejection, brokenness, and everything you've encountered in your life. This life has caused us to pick up the wrong bag and carry it as if it was supposed to be for us, as if it was meant for us or had our name on it.

But honestly, it was not meant for us to hold on to. Know the God that we serve can take us through *whatever* the situation may be!

We were only supposed to look at the bag or look in it, not hold it or handle it or take it with us or dress it up, add to it, engrave it, and make it a personal thing in our life. That was not the plan at all; it wasn't meant to be, but even though we pick and keep the wrong things in our life, He is still right there with us through it all. The Bible is a witness to this in Deuteronomy 31:6: "Be strong and of a good courage, fear not, nor be afraid of them: for the Lord thy God, He it is that doth go with thee; He will not fail thee, nor forsake thee."

So be it resolved that every situation that came in my life to

- kill me;
- take me out;
- cause me to fail;
- put me down;
- make me feel less of a person;
- make me think that I didn't matter; or
- force me to feel unwanted

didn't work. It failed. Be it resolved I'm still standing, and I'm still here, and I'm a better person from all of it.

This uncontrolled spiraling caused me to be so messed up that I am just finding out that all that I had been through had something to do with the way I entered this world as an illegitimate child, abandoned by my father at birth, never having his loving touch, his kisses, and feeling his big strong hands holding me close to his heart, pushed me into many of the feelings and emotions that I lived through growing up. The rejection, the abandonment, the neglect, and so many other feelings were the beginning of my existence. These emotions caused me to be stuck for many years, but I know now that there is more to life than what I had been through.

The fact that people would say things to me that I wasn't accustom to hearing people say to each other, like I love you, you're exceptional, you're so cute, you look nice (simple things like this) people looking at me as though they wanted to say something to me about me, meant that I had to say something back to someone that in my mind didn't like me at all.

The incidents in my life had caused me to be an introvert. I felt like I was just peeping out to see if maybe I could come out, but my response would be "I don't think so." Through this I learned how to sit quietly and make no sound at all. "If they don't see me then I don't have to respond, or make eye contact, and they won't have to look at me." I hated groups of any size, but large numbers made things even worse. I could hardly breathe, and I would just want to get out of the area that the people were in. I always felt like something was about to go down whenever I was in a group of people, and I would be in the middle of it all. I blamed myself for just about everything that would come up as it must have been something I did to make those things go wrong.

Be it resolved that I can stand before people, and with God I am ok. I walk among crowds without freaking out, I can hold my head up instead of hanging it toward the ground, I am now proud to have these big, pretty eyes (which I used to hate) as the drunk man on the corner told me one day, "you have beautiful eyes". Be it resolved that fear no longer grips my heart; I no longer expect that I will be abandoned by those close to me.

Be it resolved I am no longer afraid to be complimented. Be it resolved that I am worth talking to and being around; I am rather good company. Be it resolved that I kind of like me some Freda Denise Blair—she got something going on that she's just now uncovering. Be it resolved Jesus is with me, and He loves me, and I am finding out that He really does care about what I care about. Be it resolved that I am no longer bound to all the negativity that took over my life for over forty years, but I am free from so much and I continue to work daily on those things that the Lord brings to me.

He is more than anything else in my life, He is *everything to me!*

Be it resolved that the man that I mentioned that molested me when I was eight didn't kill me. It messed me up for many years, but I'm still here stronger now than ever in this short life of mine.

I'm better, I'm good, I have joy, I am loved, I am wanted, I am even needed, I am not dirty, it wasn't my fault, I didn't cause this or make him treat me that way, I am pretty, I am ok to look at, I don't have to hide, I'm ok, it's ok for people to compliment me and not want anything from me.

It's ok for people to want to be around me, it's ok to want to get to know me, it's ok to truly be me!

Be it resolved, no-name molester (I don't know his name), I forgive you and now I understand that you had a bad hand dealt to you. I forgive you for the pain and the dysfunction that you caused me. I choose not to take the route you did in inflicting pain on others. Instead, the Lord has shown me how to love and to be loved, and this hasn't always been easy, but look at me now. From where I was? Shewww! This was a miracle: nobody but God. Thank you, Jesus, for loving me and showing me how to love. Be it resolved, I pray that my children, and my husband have completely forgiven me for all I took them through while I was hurting, in deep pain, giving out what had been thrown on me, even finding out that I had things taken from me that I had no control of, being afraid to genuinely loving and being loved completely because of my fear of being rejected and abandoned by my own family.

I pray that you all have forgiven me. God has healed me enough from so much junk and stuff, but I am still being healed. This is indeed a process that you must continue in and trust God through it all. I pray that you know and can feel my deep love for each of you! I pray for you always that your families will not be affected by my pain and that you all will have the best families. I pray that healing has come to each of you as it has to me. I pray that even though you were given a mother with many issues, that this won't enter your home. One thing is for sure: we have broken many of our family's generational curses, and we will continue with the help of the Lord.

So, to my family, be it resolved that we will make it together, we will help your kids (my grands) to be better than we were. Be it resolved healing is coming to your house!

John 14:13–14 tells us, "Whatsoever you shall ask in my name will I do, that the Father may be glorified in the Son. If ye shall ask anything in my name, I will do it."

The things our great-grandparents, grandparents, mother, and father did that we inherited and have walked in unaware are gone in Jesus' name! Be it resolved generational curses are gone in Jesus' name!

Be it resolved we are more than conquerors in Jesus Christ, who is our healer,

- way maker
- way out
- deliverer

- protection
- guide
- escape
- hiding place
- Shepherd
- mind regulator
- heart fixer
- stabilizer
- Resurrection of our life
- El Shaddai (Lord God Almighty)
- El Elyon (The Most High God)
- Yahweh (Lord Jehovah)
- Jehovah Nissi (The Lord My Banner)
- Jehovah Raah (The Lord My Shepherd)
- Jehovah Rapha (The Lord That Heals),
- Jehovah Shammah (The Lord That is There)
- Jehovah Tsidkenu (The Lord Our Righteousness)
- Jehovah Mekoddishkem (The Lord Who Sanctifies You)
- EL Olam (The Everlasting God)
- Elohim (God)
- Jehovah Jireh (The Lord Will Provide)
- Jehovah Sabaoth (The Lord of Hosts)
- Alpha and Omega, the beginning and the End of all things.

Be it resolved we have everything we need to get through what seems to be holding us back. We have the creator of all things on our side working with us! He is the answer! Be it resolved.

The plans the enemy had and set up for my fall didn't work; I am yet standing and trusting in my Father and Savior, my help, my *victory*.

PSALM 144:1 says, "Blessed be the Lord my strength, which teacheth my hands to war, and my fingers to fight."

We will make it with what we have to use (Jesus). He's teaching me how to make it through the troubles of this world.

John 16:33 says, "I have told you these things, so that in me you may have peace, in this world you will have trouble. But take heart! I have overcome the world."

He is everything that you and I will ever need! Be it resolved we need Jesus for all this.

Chapter 9: Be It Resolved

Journal a resolution to someone that has caused the pain in your life and end that chapter today.

Chapter 10

The Mind of Being Grateful (My Bag of Gratitude)

I have been in a place of being ungrateful for the things that I have been blessed with and feeling like I was entitled to things I didn't have.

I'm not sure what it was if anyone or anything at all but my selfish self.

But I have learned down through the years that we don't have to have what we are blessed with; that's why it's a blessing, not an entitlement!

God is so faithful in shining the light where we need to wake up and smell the coffee.

At times, that same ungrateful heart comes back to spend time with me.

I now need to carry a new bag, one that will hold my gratefulness and reminders of where I came from.

There are things that the Lord allows to happen in our life to bring us back to reality.

He will allow us to go through places in our life to help us get what He is trying to show us.

My family went through a pretty rough time for several years, and we couldn't figure out what it was all about, but today as I begin to look back over my life and see where the Lord has brought us from, I can truly say I am so very grateful!

God has been very good to me and to mine. We had a very bad leak in our home for some time. Thinking that it was in the bathroom, we had it fixed and figured that we got it all and we never thought about it anymore, but that leak had damaged our hallway floor, so we arranged to have the floors repaired. The flooring guys came and pulled the floors up in the hallway, and to our surprise the floor had rotted underneath the wood flooring so much so that one of the young guy's foot went through the floor. That could have been one of us and we could have hurt ourselves very badly. But God!

Then they checked the kitchen floor to see if by chance something else was leaking there, and lo and behold the back of the refrigerator where the ice machine was connected was leaking (this was the day everything changed for us, and we knew that God was with us) we had to turn the water off (gratefulness began this very day)

When you reach to turn on the water and it doesn't respond to the command that was given, then you realize what you are blessed to have. I never realized how much we use water and how much we turn it on in a day (just grateful).

We then had to make reservations to stay in a hotel, thinking it was for a very short time, and we ended up staying for about six weeks. I took my bag of gratefulness right on out and thanked the Lord thank you for being able to have a place to lay our heads. Grateful!

At times, we just need to have what I call a thank you fit!

Or throw a thank you tantrum. You know, like kids do to get their way when they fall out on the floor. I'm saying since God didn't give us what we deserve, we should lay out and think of the goodness of Jesus; we got what we wanted but not what we deserved!

For He loves us that much to continue to bless us. We need to have a thank you fit; just go off thanking Him for all the things you've never thanked Him for before. "Lord, I thank you for my life, my health, my strength, my good days and my bad." Thank Him for your eyes, nose, and mouth. Thank Him for whatever you've been blessed with because there is always someone that wishes they could be you or have what you haven't thanked Him for! Thank you, thank you, thank you!

I believe the Lord is waiting on us to be grateful just like the word of God tells us in Luke 17:11–19 that Jesus healed ten men with leprosy but only one came back to tell Him thanks. Jesus questions the leper and ask, "Wasn't there ten?" Have you ever thought about how many times He has waited on us to come back and say thank you?

Didn't I give them what they asked me for? Didn't I answer their prayer?"

Let's get a bag of gratitude and be grateful for all the Lord has truly blessed us with, for He is worthy of all praise and thanksgiving. No one else is worthy!

Where are they, are you one of the ones that need to be thankful?

Let's get a bag of gratitude! We must live grateful lives!

Chapter 10 "The Mind of Being Grateful"

Journal using Lord I just want to Thank you for: and write all the things that you are grateful for.

I Thessalonians 5:18 "In everything give thanks: for this is the will of God in Christ Jesus concerning you."

Continue to journal. This is what helped me through some of my roughest times. It also helps to empty out all that junk that we tend to hold on to. Prayer, fasting, and counseling with someone that you can trust helps the healing process. It is a process, and healing takes time. Let the journey begin. I hope this book has helped you in some way.

Prayers and love to all that will read and be healed.
The Bag Lady Play
By Freda D Blair

There are things in our life that we tend to hide or just keep as secrets.

Every one of us has a story, a testimony, an issue, a problem, a hurt, a pain, or a disappointment. We all deal with the same types of things; we just name them differently.

We all have a past that we may or may not be very proud of. Things happen that change our future and cause our life to take unwanted detours. We often question, "Why, Lord? Why would this happen to me?"

"Where It All Started"

This is how *The Bag Lady* came to be. I once was that person wondering, "Why me?" with tear-stained eyes asking God why this had to happen to me at the tender age of eight, right after losing my dad, who was murdered just a few feet from our apartment.

We moved from the area where he was shot and killed, thinking we were going to be in a better place, only to later find out that the new place was no better than the place we had left.

My story begins with a little country store right across from our new house, which everyone in the neighborhood would shop at.

There was an old man that lived directly behind the store. He would stand out on the corner watching and speaking to everyone, seeming to be so kind and sweet. Little did I know that I would become his victim. I feel that he had done this before because he knew just what to say and do to get my undivided attention.

I would just visit the store, looking to see if our little pennies would buy anything at all. We didn't buy much because we were quite poor and didn't have enough to buy anything extra.

So, before we would or could buy, we would go to look and add up what we needed to buy a sucker or Tootsie Roll.

We did this quite often, not realizing that this nice (nice-nasty) man was watching and premeditating his actions of pulling me into his nasty world.

I loved gum and Blow Pops like most kids do today. I loved to blow bubbles and crack those suckers until the gum came out, so there I was one day looking with no real intention to buy because I didn't have any money, and the nice-nasty man was watching as he always would.

He walked over to me after I had left the store and offered me the very thing I couldn't buy—Blow Pops. He said, "I have some more at the house. If you come with me, I'll give you more."

Boy my eyes got big, and joy filled my little heart. I felt so happy about what I thought I was about to get. He most certainly did have more Blow Pops and gum at his house seemingly just waiting for me. It was all a nasty setup to get me in his house to do what he wanted to with me.

He set me up only to molest me. This changed my life forever. My life as I knew it was gone, it was over. I went home and told no one because I knew I was in trouble for following him to his house in the first place.

I never mentioned what happened, and I pushed it as far back as I could, never to remember it again until the age of forty-nine, when I went on a sabbatical after becoming a pastor, asking for directions for the church and asking the Lord to show me what was wrong and to help me and not allow me to go back as I came. I wanted to be free of whatever I was dealing with, and while praying God showed me a film-like vision of my young life and the molestation that took place. I lay crying, screaming into a pillow so that the neighbors in the next hotel room couldn't hear me.

This was the start of my own bags being opened, bags that I didn't know I had, bags of being molested, bags of rejections, bags of abandonment, low self-esteem, feeling unlovable, unattractive, unwanted, feelings that it was all my fault, not knowing how to love or be loved, thinking that I was nothing and nobody.

I was drowning in self-pity, I was very shy, timid, and afraid to be whoever I was supposed to be, that I literally would freak out at times because I was being looked at.

After leaving the mountain and receiving counseling and prayer and praying myself, seeking to be healed and seeking Him to help me forgive a man whose name I never knew; I didn't know if he was even alive anymore, but I didn't want him to have control of me anymore. My life was a mess, and I needed God to fix me.

I could see my life changing right before my eyes. Forgiveness sets you free and helps you become whole.

Don't ever think that this is an overnight healing because it's not; it's a process, and the process can take as long as you allow it to. It truly depends on what you are willing to do to move forward and to be free of your past.

Remember that there is not one thing you can change about your past, but you can direct your future with the help of the Lord Jesus Christ. He will lead you into all truth and righteousness; there is a better life and a better way for you to move in and that life is right before you when you decide to make that move out of your stinking past.

Let the past be just what it is: your yesterday. Don't drag that into your brand-spanking-new tomorrow, which isn't promised to us any way, so if you are blessed to see it, ask the Lord, "What can I do for you today?"

Watch where your life ends up—better than you can even imagine.

God began to strategically give me *The Bag Lady*. The Bag Lady was raped, molested, abused, abandoned, broken, mistreated, and so much more; she is completely messed up.

The Bag Lady carries many bags to disguise herself in public. She carries with her all the things that have happened to her: all the rejected situations, the denials, the guilt and shame, the "I am nothing, and will never be," "I'm ugly" syndrome, the "I can't do anything right" attitude, the "I wish I was someone else because their life looks better", the "no one wants me, can't please anyone if I tried" mentality.

*This has been a one person play, but you may have as many as you'd like to use, also change clothes to look like each age.

Scene 1
Playhouse

Do you remember when you were young and playing house was the thing to do? It was fun playing with your dolls, and you were the mommy, and you took care of your baby doll as you were being taking care of.

It was fun to talk to your dolls and let them know when they were good girls or being bad, dressing them up and taking them with you on your hip, walking around as if you were the one in control.

This is the scene in an eight-year-old girl's life, thinking that she gets a chance to play this little fun game with her daddy, that special man in her life, the very first man she ever loved, the one that promised to take care of her and to make her feel secure just because he's there. He was the one to provide, love, keep and help her become that woman he would be proud of and one that she would look back and be proud to say, "That's my dad."

The scene is an eight-year-old frail little girl who is being molested and the changes that she will deal with.

She is sitting in her room when her dad enters. He says to her, "Do you want to play mom and dad?" And she responds, "Ok, Daddy, that will be fun." (She excitedly skips across the room.)

> Dad: Ok, let's pretend that you are the mom, and I am the dad, and we are married.
> Little girl: Ok, Daddy.
> Dad: You lay on the bed.
> Little girl: Ok, Daddy.
> Dad: I'm going to tickle you, ok?
> Little girl: Ok.
> Dad: This is fun, isn't it?

Little girl: Yes, Daddy. (She is laughing because he really is tickling her.)
Dad: Yes, it's fun.
Little girl: (laughing)
Dad: This feels good too.
Little girl: Ouch, Daddy, that hurts. I don't want to play this game anymore.
Dad: It's ok. It will hurt at first, but remember that you're the mommy. Don't you want to be the mommy?
Little girl: (with tears) No, Daddy, no!

Scene 2
Sexual Too Young

The nine-year-old is in her room hiding under her covers when her dad enters the dark room.
Little girl: I don't want to play. No, Daddy, no!
The molestation continues day after day.

Scene 3
Orally Wrong

The girl is eleven years old now. Things are changing; he is trying new things.
Little girl: No, Daddy, no! You're really hurting me!
Dad: Shut up! You started this little game, and you know you like it.
Little girl: Please stop.

Dad: Shut up before I beat yo' tail—and you better not tell anyone. If you do, they will take you away. This is our little secret. I love you.

Scene 4

The girl is now fifteen years old. He's getting on top of her.
Teenage girl: No, Daddy, no! This isn't right!
Dad: Shut your mouth! You're mine.
Teenage girl: Dad, please don't do this. What if I get pregnant?
Dad: Then we will put you out of here.
Teenage girl: Please stop.

About the Author

Freda Blair is the senior pastor of Christ Temple Apostolic Church of Winchester, Kentucky. She is a teacher at Grace School of Ministry and a certified Chaplain, she is a Life Coach and a Biblical Counselor. She is an ordained pastor with the Pentecostal Assemblies of the World, Inc., as well as a District Elder with the First Apostolic Council of Kentucky and Tennessee.

Pastor Blair has a passion for women who have been broken, in which she is blessed to be available to be used by the Lord to help through her ministry. Out of her lived experiences she birthed the Broken Pieces Annual Women's Retreat. As the founder and visionary of the Broken Pieces Ministry, she has purposed and positioned herself to speak life into as many women as possible during what is referred to as the "Mountain Experience." From this ministry, Pastor Blair brought to life the play known as *The Bag Lady*. This play has helped women see their past standing before them and helps begin their healing during the annual retreats.

The Broken Pieces Women's Retreat is held each year in Pigeon Forge, Tennessee, and has drawn hundreds of women from various states, backgrounds, religious foundations, and life experiences.

Pastor Blair is a pivotal voice in the Kingdom of God. It is evident that God is using her to help build His Kingdom in this millennium. Lives are being empowered and changed.

www.ingramcontent.com/pod-product-compliance
Ingram Content Group UK Ltd.
Pitfield, Milton Keynes, MK11 3LW, UK
UKHW022210230426
12048UKWH00016BA/767

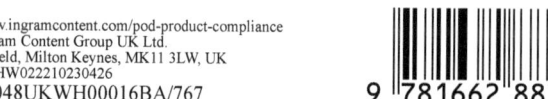